This book is dedicated to Elizabeth Baker
for her valuable help in weaving my
ideas into literary logic… to Kate for her
unwavering support in more ways than
there are pages in this book… to all
those lost souls who are only momentarily
side-tracked.

No More Alps
©2013 Bill Calhoun

Self published edition 2013

Editor: Rebekah McGrady
Cover design and art: E-source; e-sourcemedia.com
Interior illustrations and design: Rebekah McGrady

ISBN 978-981-07-7035-8

Printed by CreateSpace

NO MORE ALPS

BILL CALHOUN

Contents

About the Author

Bill Calhoun is an award winning American producer, director and choreographer. As an international speaker for over 16 years, Bill has been delivering dynamic presentations and training to diverse multicultural audiences. Now he brings his experience and enthusiasm directly to YOU. In order to succeed, he explains, you must focus on developing yourself and creating a strong, charismatic personality. In this book, Bill will teach you how to effectively:

- Cultivate self-confidence

- Tap into your imagination as a rich source of strength

- Offer daily affirmations to guide and inspire you

- Instill self-assurance to empower innovation and creativity

Introduction/Preface

The purpose of this book is to inspire by means of building your self- confidence and by allowing yourself to dream BIG. So many of us today live a life that is incomplete. Not because we don't have what it takes, but because we are restricted by our own self-limiting thoughts and actions. The building of self-confidence is not hard, but it does require some effort. There is no need for exerting yourself to extremes here...simply read the material, absorb it and then...**make it happen.**

Think of the story of the man who tried to jump over a hill. He went a long way back, he thought about how he was going to tackle that hill head on. Then ran so hard towards the hill that by the time he got there, he was out of steam and had to lie down to rest. You know what happened next? He got up and walked over the hill. So many people spend all of their time preparing, but never achieving. If you want to run, then prepare yourself to run and race across that finish line!

Now that you've decided you want to build your self-confidence, you should resolve to follow it all the way through to the end. Know this—no halfhearted weak effort will help you achieve your life's purpose. Go forward with the knowledge that you can and will achieve all that you desire and much will come of your energy and perseverance.

Bill Calhoun
May 2013

Chapter 1
Power of the Will

The importance of will power is recognized by most of us, yet we hardly ever give any thought or effort to developing it. Did you even know that you could develop your will power? Ask yourself this: why do we strive harder towards one goal over another? How do we go about building and then—more importantly—directing our will power?

There are many things in life we want to avoid such as pain, poverty and ill health. We tend to put a lot of emphasis on staying ahead of those pitfalls. On the other side, there are many things we very much want to achieve such as wealth, power, knowledge and independence. What helps us determine what we should go for and what we must avoid? Our will power: the power of our desire to either achieve or avoid those situations.

If you were to tell me that you wanted to become the greatest performer and take the world by storm, then I would ask you a few questions: How strong is your desire to be the world's greatest performer? Will you practice regularly? Will you put forth your best effort to achieve your dreams? If you answer by telling me that you may not be able to put all of your effort into it because your days are super busy, then I would point out that your desire is not strong enough to make you the world's greatest performer.

This applies to YOU, who are in search of a quick way to build your self-confidence. How strong is your desire to develop this great power? Is it strong enough to lead you carefully through the guide, reading the suggestions AND putting them into practice? Are you willing to make reasonable sacrifices in order to achieve your goals? Your answers to these questions will determine what your success will be. There are a few times in life when we suddenly realize all things are possible. We resolve to achieve better and greater things than ever before but after a little while, the feeling begins to fade away and we are left with only a wisp of a reminder that we wanted more for ourselves as we accept less. Here are some tips on how you can seize this very moment—whatever you can do or dream, you can begin today.

- Before acting impulsively on every whim that comes into your head, make a habit of considering the advantages, dangers and probabilities before deciding

There are
a few times
in life when
we suddenly
realize all
things are
possible.

which way to go. Making a "pros and cons" list can spare you from making a serious mistake.

- Sometimes an idea must be repeated many times before it makes an impression on your mind. Think of advertising or that song that keeps playing on the radio—with repeated exposure, it can quickly become a part of your daily routine! The same is true of repeating affirmations to yourself. The more you say them, the more they will become a part of who you are.

- Be careful of the influences around you. While it is always a good idea to seek advice from those you trust and who understand you, once the advice has been considered, it is up to you to pursue the next step.

- Make a point of being as honest with yourself as you are with others. Advise yourself as you would a good friend.

- Recognize that you owe it to yourself to make the most of your life here and now. You are unique and only you can do what you were put here to do.

- Get in the habit of addressing situations as they arise, rather than putting off making choices. Instead of letting all those good ideas in your mind lie around, waiting to take hold, put them in their proper places.

If there is something you can do about it, do it—if not, deal with it and move on.

- To begin is half the battle. It is so easy to put off, waiting until tomorrow but before you know it, life will have passed you by. Just by taking that first step to achieving your dreams, you have already succeeded.

- Have you heard the expression, "Where there's a will, there's a way?" This shows how important will power is in getting you through the process. Be encouraged to keep going, despite obstacles, failures or setbacks. After all, if it is too easy, it may not be worth winning!

The great and powerful force of your will makes your life what it is! There is practically no limit to building your self-confidence once you set your mind to it.

Chapter 2
Cultivate Self-Confidence

A self-confident manner is developed by paying attention to many different aspects of what makes you who you are—through your speech and mannerisms, to how you think and carry yourself. People pick up on your level of self-confidence by what you choose to say, how you say it and what actions you take. The four most important areas in which you can begin to develop your self-confidence are speech, thought, action and mannerisms. Follow these guidelines and in no time, you will be talking the talk AND walking the walk!

Speech

The way you speak offers a quick view into how you feel about yourself and what you have to say. You should always aim to speak with confidence, to deliver your words with a sincere expression of your thoughts. When you really know what you're talking about, it shows in the words you use and your entire personality. So how do you cultivate sincerity in your conversations? Begin with these tips:

- Speak when you have something to say; don't just talk to hear the sound of your own voice.

- Concentrate on the subject you're discussing and speak with conviction.

- Pay attention, listen to what others are saying and then respond.

- Take a few deep breaths before you speak—breathing affects your attitude! Get in the habit of doing some deep breathing throughout the day and you will soon find that your speech comes across as calm, assured and full of self-confidence.

Thought

Nothing leads to hesitation and embarrassment like opening your mouth and not having a clue as to what you're going to say! In order to appear self-confident, you shouldn't guess, imagine or even take for granted what you will say—you should know.

- Imagine that your mind is a machine; a machine you have control over. I know it is easy to lose focus and let your thoughts drift. If your mind is prone to wandering, go after it and bring it back!

- Constantly hold yourself in high esteem. This doesn't mean to consider yourself better than everybody else, just remind yourself that you are no greater than the sum of your thoughts.

- Your mind is a fertile place for all kinds of thoughts to grow—both good and bad. If you allow negative thoughts to take up too much space in your mind, you may become discouraged and lose confidence. Get in the habit of repeating daily affirmations so that positive thoughts crowd out the bad ones.

Action

Do you ever find yourself worrying about what others will think or say about you? If you are constantly seeing yourself through someone else's eyes, it may cause you to lose motivation and confidence.

- Try not to focus on what other people may or may not be thinking of you. This hypersensitivity will only eat away at your self-confidence over time.

- Be confident and stand firm in your beliefs.

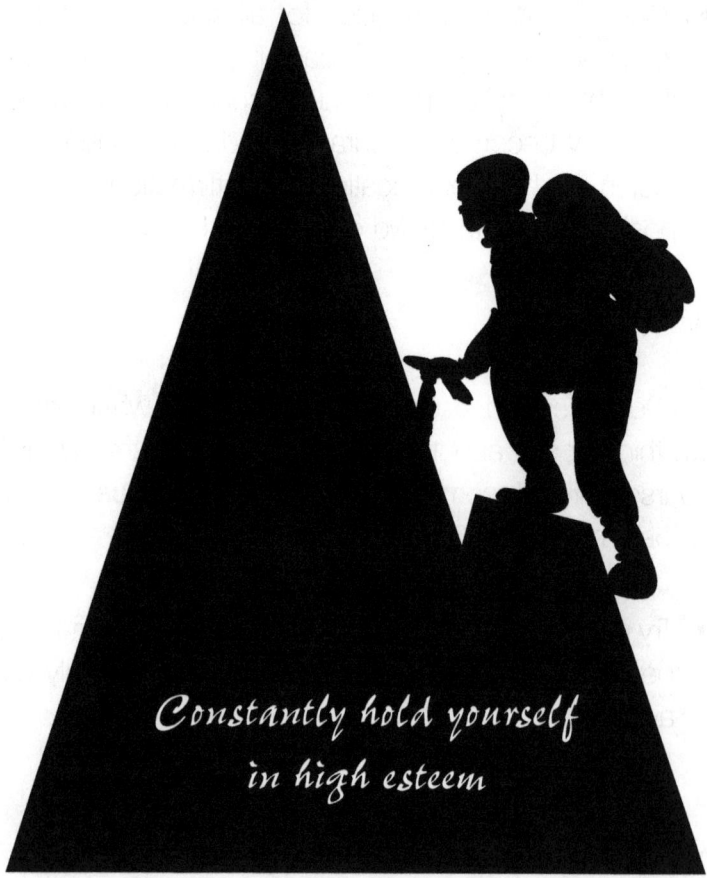

Constantly hold yourself
in high esteem

- Pay attention to whether your audience understands what you are saying or doing. Look for visual cues and stay tuned to the feedback others unconsciously provide.

Mannerisms

How do you greet the world each day? Do you wake up ready to take on the challenges and opportunities that await you or do you sit back and wait for life to happen to you? How you present yourself will have a significant impact on both the impression you make on others and how you perceive yourself.

- Giving in to self-consciousness can make you do things you don't want to do; say yes when you want to say no. In short, it can rob you of your power and individuality.

- Probably every single person has at one time or another had feelings of nervousness or anxiety—one of the best ways to combat these feelings is to fully immerse yourself into a project you care about or focus on the welfare of others. By doing this, you can distract yourself from any anxiety and uneasiness.

- The most important thing you can do to help your body communicate effectively, is be yourself. The emphasis should be on the sharing of ideas, not on the performance.

- Strive to be as genuine and natural as you are when you speak to family members and friends.

- Smile before you even say a word and greet everyone you meet with a firm handshake.

Chapter 3
Power of Positive Thinking

You should never have to apologize for yourself. Now you may be asking, what does that mean? What it refers to is the habit we can often get into where we find ourselves making excuses for the things we say or do (or don't say or do). Developing your self-confidence will allow you to overcome the daily (maybe hourly!) streams of negative thoughts that come into your mind that can potentially shut you down.

If you find yourself constantly bombarded with thoughts of failure, you will surely set yourself up to fail. You must work on developing the habit of positive thinking—of seeing yourself as someone who is capable of great things—because as your mind believes, so you become. In order to turn the mind toward the positive, some inner work is required, since attitude and thoughts do not change overnight.

15

When you find negative thoughts taking over, ask yourself these questions: How does negative thinking work for me? Do I feel encouraged when I surround myself with thoughts/attitudes that bring me down? Would I rather be discontent or content? Your answers to these questions will help highlight the power of your thoughts and how they are capable of shaping your life. These tips and techniques will allow you to harness the power of positive thinking. Try them—you have nothing to lose and everything to gain!

- Use your imagination to see only good and beneficial aspects of a situation. When you find yourself overwhelmed by a negative thought or emotion, take a deep breath and visualize any favorable aspect of the circumstance.

- Focus on using only positive words, both with yourself and when you are speaking with others. Positive thoughts are constructive, so avoid using negative words such as, "weak, failure or lack." Instead say to yourself, "I am confident, I am strong, I am able!"

- The habit of positive thinking, once it has taken root, can become a source of attraction. What you put out there is what comes back to you. You will discover that the power of a single thought at the beginning of the day can have a long lasting effect. It can change despair into hope and fear into courage. It can give you strength and resolve and set in motion an influence

that will reach to the ends of the earth.

- Try meditation in order to help you focus your thoughts. Developing the habit of constant and searching reflection will serve you for a lifetime. Think of it as a chance to "sleep on it." Giving your thoughts time to mature will play a big part in building your mind.

- It is a good idea to think out loud when you are alone. In this way, you are able to get your thoughts out into concrete form. It may seem silly at first, but there is an advantage to hearing your own thoughts spoken aloud. You get an impression of the sound of the words, for how they come together. Your thoughts, when stated out loud, take on a life of their own! They can then be better analyzed, considered and re-shaped. The very act of giving expression to your thoughts invests them with new power and importance.

- Positive thinking does more than affect our lives on a daily basis. While our thoughts are building our character, they also play a part in shaping human destiny. Just imagine: the thoughts you have today could have an effect on future generations! We should not strive to perform one great act of courage but courageously perform all acts, however small our everyday life.

- A person who focuses on positive thinking is a cheerful thinker. This means you are an optimist, one who sees nothing but good in himself and the world around him. You have learned how to be selective in your thinking, knowing what is good and rejecting the bad. You use your thoughts to clarify and brighten the lives of others. Robert Louis Stevenson once wrote, "A happy man or woman is a great thing to find…he or she is a radiating force of good will and their entrance into a room is as though another candle has been lighted."

- Positive thinking should always lead to action. You may tell yourself all day that you are cheerful and courageous, but if you sit in a corner by yourself and do nothing, you have simply deluded yourself. It is not enough that you believe what you think; you must be it, live it and act it!

When you focus on positive thinking, your attitude begins to change and you will find yourself more positive, strong and constructive. You will move forward in life expecting good things, with hope and enthusiasm for what lies ahead. The result of your persistent, positive thinking will be that you are thought of as a happy and successful person.

It can happen every day, at the beginning of your day. A single positive thought enters your mind and begins its wonderful work. This thought leads to another and another and soon you realize things aren't so bad after all. This will give you courage to take the next step and suddenly, your horizons will widen, your interests will grow and by doing this day in and day out, you will change your entire life. Those petty concerns that come up will no longer be seen as setbacks, but rather an inevitable part of life. You will welcome them as the opportunities they are—for personal growth and self-development!

"A happy man or woman is a great thing to find…he or she is a radiating force of good will and their entrance into a room is as though another candle has been lighted."

21

Chapter 4
Power of Imagination

Every great work in the world has first had its place in the human imagination. If you want to build a bench, you must first picture in your mind the kind of bench it should be. Likewise, every artist or CEO can trace in his or her imagination an image or idea of what would eventually become a product or a service or an empire.

Think of your imagination as a gallery filled with pictures — not hung with masterpieces from famous artists, but with images of those things you have done and what you want to do. You may not turn all of these pictures into realities at once, but they are there to encourage and inspire you along the way.

In your imagination lies the difference between a timid,

shy person and one who is self-confident. While one pictures defeat and failure, the other sees him or herself as a winner. If your imagination is filled with pictures of all the ways in which you will fail, those images will only haunt you day and night. If instead, when you search your imagination and only find ways in which success will be found and achieved, then you have in place a very powerful reminder in front of you. This image will serve as a powerful reminder, offering joy by day and something to dream about at night.

Few people realize how important a part imagination plays in our everyday lives. A business executive must give a prospective customer a mental picture of the services offered by the products he sells. The doctor describes for her patient an image of what surgery she will perform and what the outcome will look like. The politician describes the condition of how things will be once he is elected into office. The public speaker illuminates and illustrates his subject by capturing the audience's imagination. So in every activity the order is always to paint a mental picture first, then follow it up with an action.

Strive to surround yourself with people and experiences that will inspire and encourage you to develop the best parts of yourself. Don't be limited by what is around you; seek out inspiration everywhere you go.

Don't be limited by what is around you; seek out inspiration everywhere you go.

Chapter 5
Building Confidence

There is something about a self-confident person that you notice immediately. You may not know exactly what it is—you can't quite put your finger on the specifics, but you know it when you see it. A self-confident person is poised; looks you straight in the eye and speaks in a voice that is calm and direct. They are sure of themselves and are effortlessly able to command your attention and approval. When you are self-confident, you silently communicate that fact to the world around you. There are different ways to do this through many qualities, including:

Politeness

This is one of the most valuable assets in any situation. It is a mistake to think of simple good manners as weak or unimportant. The strongest and bravest among us have been known for the courtesy and respect that they show everyone in their lives. There is no situation, either in your professional or personal life that is not made better by being polite and having pleasing manners.

Self-expression

Pay attention to how you convey yourself. You unconsciously communicate every day. You attract or repel with your voice, a look, your gestures, the way you walk and your appearance. Think of yourself as a positive and magnetic force and face the day strongly and bravely.

Generosity

Remind yourself every day to make the most of your time and of yourself. Give to those who are in need and do not stoop to do a mean thing. Be grateful for the blessings you have and the unique gift that only you can bring to this world.

Gentleness

Work on exuding this controlled strength. A strong, powerful personality does not move through the world in jerks but in smooth curves. Violence is weakness, it is an admission of inferiority and repels where it aims to

Be
grateful
for the
blessings you
have and the
unique gift that only
you can bring to this
world.

control. Be conscious of your power and you will never have to display it in a forceful way.

When you are able to express your self-assurance through these qualities, you are truly expressing the inward realization of your self-confidence. When you see yourself as self-confident, self-respecting, strong, gentle and polite, the world will see you that way too.

Chapter 6
Daily Affirmations

Here is a daily plan that you can put into place right now to help you build self-confidence. You can begin on any day of the month, with the lesson assigned for that day and continue to repeat the entire series for as long as necessary. Each day consists of a focus—an important characteristic, followed by a series of affirmations.

Day 1:

Poise—composure; controlled grace in motion; avoid any nervous or unnecessary movements of your body and mind; remain calm, peaceful and deliberate.

Repeat to yourself:

Poise gives power

Poise gives purpose

Poise offers possibilities

Poise strengthens my thoughts

Day 2:

Optimism—seeing the bright side of life, choosing to see that the glass is half-full instead of half-empty; believe that today is yours.

Dwell on these thoughts:

A smile disarms anger and discontent

What I look for, I will find

The best time to be happy is right now

I can make the world a better place

Day 3:

Wisdom—develop common sense; observe closely; think before you speak with the aim for accurate judgments; grow daily in discernment.

Think deeply on these thoughts:

Wisdom is better than riches

To know better is to do better

To know is to conquer

I am as great as my thoughts

<u>Day 4:</u>

Earnestness—be eager to achieve; get the best by doing your best; be sincere, become interested and determined; feel strong and active.

Say these purposefully:

I only do one thing at a time

My happiness grows out of earnestness and sincerity

There are no limits or boundaries to what I can do

Day 5:

Realization—ask yourself: what abilities do I have? What can I do best? How can I use my skills to make the world a better place? What do I need to work on? The answers to these questions will help you discern what to work on and how to apply your unique talents in bigger and better ways!

Study these thoughts:

I know what I am

My thoughts and actions can achieve wonders

I realize my power for great achievement

My abilities grow as I use and refine them

Day 6:

Patience — you have the capacity for waiting which gains you self-respect and the goodwill of others; maintaining a calm exterior under any circumstance will greatly increase your power; decide to be kind, polite and thoughtful.

Repeat the following several times with great care:

Patience gives me power

Patience overcomes difficulty

Patience wins friends and influences others

Patience is a virtue

Day 7:

Deliberateness—carefully weigh each fact; think deeply and reflect often; look before you leap; take all the time you need, think and speak intentionally.

Say these thoughts out loud:

Think before you speak

Weigh things carefully—to weigh well is to do well

Foresight is always better than afterthought

Haste makes waste

Day 8:

Faith—all power comes from faith, a belief or trust; faith bridges difficulties and accomplishes the seemingly impossible; through faith you can say with assurance, "I can and I will."

Concentrate on these thoughts:

Faith can move mountains

Faith has always inspired great minds

Faith is evidence of things not seen

Faith replaces fear and points the way forward

Day 9:

Unselfishness—be generous and kind; give to others; with daily acts of kindness and words of encouragement, make those around you happy.

Think deeply on these:

It is more blessed to give than to receive

To give much is to have much

I am thoughtful to all those who come in contact with me

Today I will do at least one random act of kindness

Day 10:

Punctual—be up and going, doing everything on time; be prompt in your actions and punctual to every appointment, you will find that time flies.

Repeat these phrases with a positive attitude:

He who hesitates is lost

Procrastination will only steal my precious time

I will do everything on time

Finish today's business today

Day 11:

Health—a strong mind and a strong body is the ideal combination; finding joy in your work will daily strengthen you; develop endurance.

Hold in your mind the positive thoughts of having perfect health:

Breathe deeply

Get a good night's sleep

Exercise regularly

Schedule a break—have some playtime every day

Day 12:

Silence—decide to listen more than you speak today; silence gives time for thoughts to grow and deepen; your reserve gives the impression of power.

Silently think about these:

Still waters run deep

Real growth in the world is silent and gradual

Talk the most and you learn the least

Human beings were given two ears and one mouth for a reason

Day 13:

Self-Confidence—assurance, boldness, initiative and independence, claim your own right now; be self-reliant and know that you can do all things.

Say these boldly:

Self-confidence is essential to success

I rely wholeheartedly on myself

My self-confidence grows daily

I have a high estimate of myself

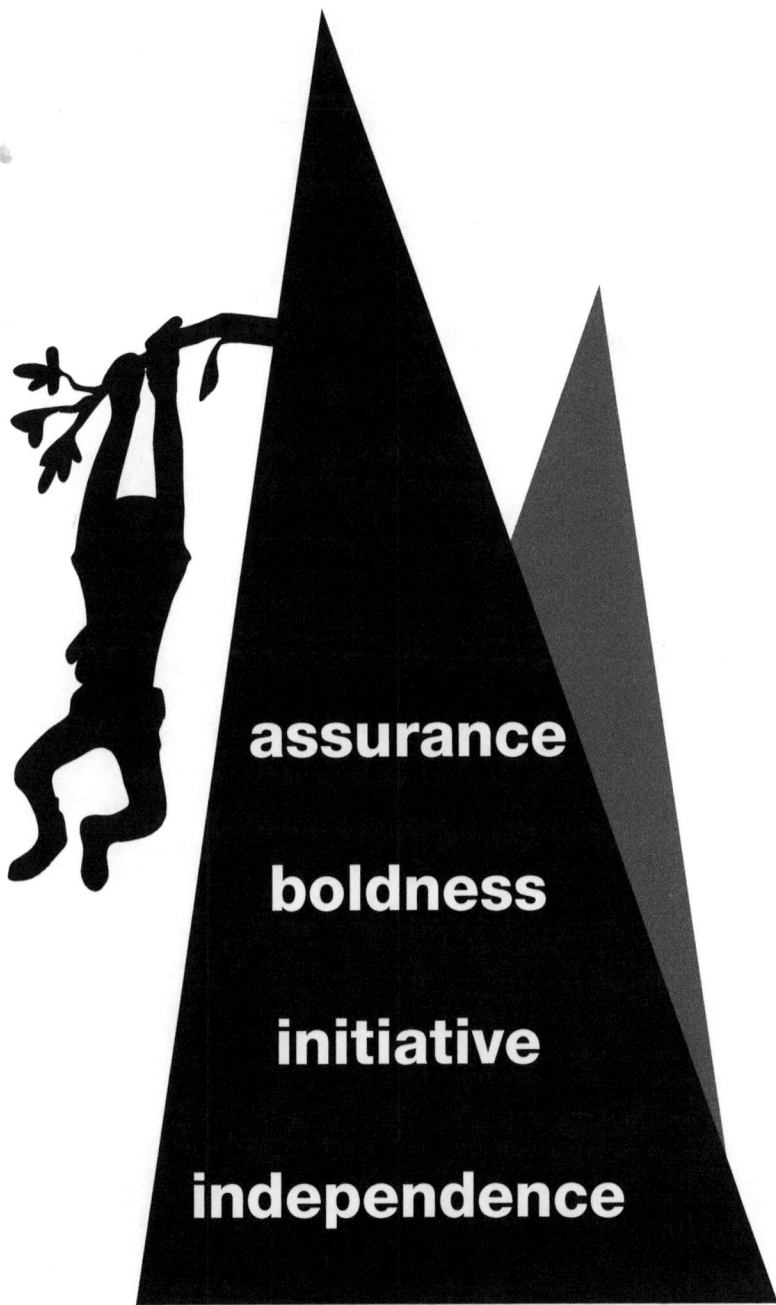

assurance

boldness

initiative

independence

Day 14:

Sincerity—be truthful in your thoughts and speech; this will show in the way you carry yourself, what you do and how you conduct your life.

Affirm these with great sincerity:

Say what you mean and mean what you say

Do everything thoroughly

What the heart thinks, let the tongue speak

Do not exaggerate or misstate

Day 15:

Concentration — fix it in your mind to do one thing at a time; be interested in what you do; take new responsibilities and apply yourself persistently.

Hold these thoughts in your mind:

I will do one thing at a time today, giving my full attention every time

Plan all work out as well as you can

Avoid anything that distracts

Concentrate with all your power

Day 16:

Love — the greatest gift you can give; it means sympathy and a willingness to sacrifice for others; let your heart go out to all.

Repeat these sincerely:

Love sacrifices all things

I love my neighbor as myself

Accept love as the greatest gift of all – don't be afraid to love

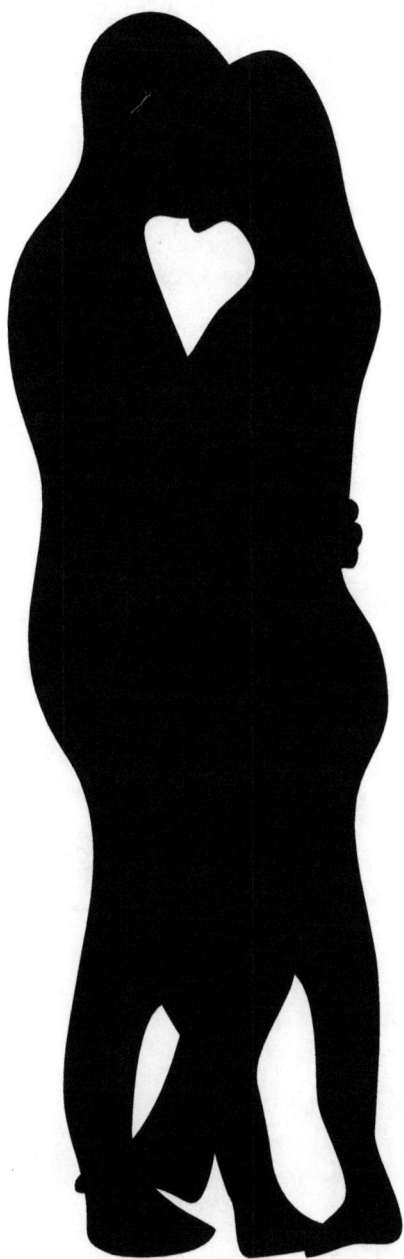

67

Day 17:

Power—become equal to great achievements; do everything with purpose and energy, put your best into all you do; become more influential every day.

Emphasize the following:

I depend on my own efforts

Persistence spells success

My power increases every day

All power is mine for the taking

Day 18:

Moderation — make the most of yourself; be strong and firm in your beliefs; do not do anything to excess, keep yourself in strong and healthy condition.

Affirm these solemnly:

Let your tastes be simple

Avoid excess in all things

Practice the art of self-control daily

Day 19:

Sympathy—feel kindly towards others, be thoughtful and tolerant; make the path smooth for others with acts of kindness and words of cheer; help others be happy.

Think on these things:

I am part of all I have met

Always be gracious towards others

Have compassion for all

Be tuned in to how others are feeling

Day 20:

Friendliness—cheerfulness wins friends; your mind will be lit up by mental sunshine and this will reflect in your face; make yourself attractive and interesting to others.

Say these words out loud with a smile on your face:

I am always cheerful

My life makes me happy and successful

I smile in the face of trouble

I am brighter and happier every day

Day 21:

Truth—think truth, speak truth and live truth; power and self-confidence come from the awareness of being right.

Repeat these words many times:

Truth is born from honesty and sincerity

I dare to be true

I love truth for truth's sake

My life and decisions I make are based on integrity

Power and self-confidence come from the awareness of being right.

Day 22:

Speech—speak deliberately and say your words clearly; let your aim be to use simple, direct words; if you do not know how to pronounce a word, look it up!

Practice these out loud:

Repeat e, a, aw, ah, o, oo

Sing the word "bell" and hold onto the "l" sound

Quickly repeat be-ba-baw-bah-bo-boo

Sharply say he, ha, haw ho, hoo

Day 23:

Duty—do the work that is in front of you and do it to the best of your ability; do it gladly and know that the reward for doing one duty is the power to do another; be inspired by a love of work done well.

Say these words positively:

I daily do my duty

I move forward every day

Responsibility is the path to success

Duty and obligation know no fear

Day 24:

Decency—cultivate an innocence and clarity in mind and body; aim for moral integrity and honor; know that a personal example can help be a role model for others.

Emphasize these thoughts:

The windows of decency are always clean

Be gracious and civil in all transactions

Practice self-restraint

Let moral respectability be a prize possession in itself

Day 25:

Certainty—an act of definite results; know exactly what you want and work towards it; decide everything carefully and push forward with determination.

Say these words with conviction:

This one thing I do

I know what I am working for

I am energetic and determined

I can and I will

Know exactly what you want and work towards it; decide everything carefully and push forward with determination

Day 26:

Integrity—let it be said of you that you are as good as your word; deal fairly and justly with everyone; keep every promise you ever make.

Repeatedly affirm these thoughts:

Honesty is the best policy

I am honest with everyone

I say what I mean and mean what I say

To lose my honor is to lose myself

Day 27:

Enthusiasm—put your inspiration to work; put your whole heart into everything you do; be doing great things right now.

Repeat these eagerly:

Nothing great was ever done without enthusiasm

I have high hopes

My enthusiasm is contagious

I will achieve

Day 28:

Justice—develop a spirit of "fair play;" stand back and take an objective view of circumstances and people; try to see others' points of view; display your full potential.

Emphasize these:

Justice is one of the greatest virtues

Justice will triumph

I will do myself justice by living up to my potential

I will be fair with everyone I meet

Justice
will
triumph

Day 29:

Tact—strive to say the right thing at the right time in the right way; try not to offend in speech or manner.

Read these carefully:

Be considerate of others

When making a decision, weigh consequences carefully

Be discreet and sensitive in personal matters

Cultivate a refined taste

Day 30:

Imagination—fill the mind with helpful, inspiring pictures; all great ideas begin in the imagination; picture the best life for yourself and make it happen.

Picture these vividly:

What kind of person do I want to be?

What great purpose do I have in life?

What do I need to get done today?

How can I change the world?

Day 31:

Personality — build a strong, charismatic personality; be strong in thought and purpose; develop the best in you.

Affirm these out loud:

I am a strong personality

I work on and develop myself every day

My power is unlimited

I am a leader

Afterward

It is never too early in life to apply personal checks and balances to your routines and processes, and likewise, it is never – even if you feel you are at your ultimate ROCK BOTTOM – never, ever too late to reassess everything, bring focus back into your life, and completely redefine and 'relaunch' yourself. Those who believe in the power of their own mind can deal a devastatingly exacting blow to the negative habits, individuals, and ideas infecting their lives, clearing the 'Old Self' away with one fell swoop!

Congratulations for completing this book! I have no doubt that you will begin seeing changes all around you very soon.

Shifting your outlook transforms the entire world around you, how others perceive and relate to you, and you will find yourself looking for a higher and higher good in your life with other positive influences who are searching for the same.

Whether you pray, chant, meditate, run, cross your fingers, or simply hold hope silently in your heart, remember to seek only those things that will add value to the person you are working so hard to become.

Climb!

Thank you!!!
Can I ask
a favor?

Thank you so much for reading my book. I hope you really liked it.

As you probably know, many people look at the reviews on Amazon before they decide to purchase a book.

If you liked the book, could you please take a minute to leave a review with your feedback?

60 seconds is all I'm asking for, and it would mean the world to me.

Thank you so much,
Bill C.

www.ingramcontent.com/pod-product-compliance
Lightning Source LLC
Chambersburg PA
CBHW071008040426
42443CB00007B/717